PEOPLE WHERE THEY ARE

Anthony Clarvoe

BROADWAY PLAY PUBLISHING INC
New York
BroadwayPlayPub.com

PEOPLE WHERE THEY ARE
© Copyright 2020 Anthony Clarvoe

Cover art by Julie Summers, courtesy of the University of Tennessee Research Foundation

First edition: November 2020
I S B N: 978-0-88145-867-1

Book design: Marie Donovan
Page make-up: Adobe InDesign
Typeface: Palatino

PEOPLE WHERE THEY ARE was originally commissioned and developed by Clarence Brown Theatre (Calvin MacLean, Producing Artistic Director; Tom Cervone, Managing Director).

The world premiere of PEOPLE WHERE THEY ARE was presented by Clarence Brown Theatre, Knoxville, Tennessee, on 2 October 2019. The cast and creative contributors were:

MRS CLARK ....Aleah Vassell
MR CARAWAN .... Owen Squire Smith
MAY .... Brittany Marie Pirozzoli
EMMA..Brenda Orellana
NED... Collin Andrews
JOHN .... Jade Arnold

Directors ....Calvin MacLean & Dee Dee Batteast
Scenic designer...Carrie Ferrelli
Lighting designer .... Bill Miller
Costume designer...John Merritt
Sound designer..Mike Ponder
Dramaturg .... Gina M Di Salvo
Choreographer/Intimacy coach ....Casey Sams
Dialect coach ....Kathy Logelin
Production manager ....Susan L McMillan
Stage manager... Dane Urban

ACKNOWLEDGMENTS

This happened because my old friend Cal MacLean asked if I would come to Tennessee. I can't imagine a more talented or a more great-hearted collaborator.

I first learned about the Highlander Folk School from the documentary film *You Got to Move*, directed by Lucy Massie Phenix and Veronica Selver. The staff of the Highlander Research and Education Center welcomed our project and were an inspiration to us, as they are to activists around the world.

The playwrights in my classes in Oakland, California, lived this history and continue to speak up for justice. I am profoundly grateful for their lessons.

The script is indebted for ideas and true stories to many books, especially: Guy and Candie Carawan, *Sing for Freedom: The Story of the Civil Rights Movement Through Its Songs*; Septima Clark (Cynthia Stokes Brown, ed.), *Ready from Within: Septima Clark & the Civil Rights Movement*; John Gaventa, *Power and Powerlessness: Quiescence and Rebellion in an Appalachian Valley*; John M. Glen, *Highlander: No Ordinary School*; Myles Horton (Dale Jacobs, ed.), *The Myles Horton Reader: Education for Social Change*; John Lewis (with Michael D'Orso), *Walking With the Wind: A Memoir of the Movement*; David Spener, *We Shall Not Be Moved (No Nos Moverán): Biography of a Song of Struggle*; Lee Staples, *Roots to Power: A Manual for Grassroots*

Organizing; Zaragosa Vargas, *Labor Rights are Civil Rights: Mexican American Workers in Twentieth-Century America*; and Eliot Wigginton, ed., *Refuse to Stand Silently By: An Oral History of Grass Roots Social Activism in America, 1921-1964.*

The faculty, administration, and staff of the University of Tennessee, Knoxville, were essential partners. My thanks to Townes Lavidge Osborn and Jennifer Banner for their generous and heartfelt support.

This play is for Clarence Brown Theatre and for the many citizens of the American South who believe that the future can and should be better than the past.

It is dedicated to Highlander and to Cal MacLean.

Nothing is possible without Kate.

CHARACTERS & SETTING

MRS CLARK, *African-American, from Charleston, South Carolina*

MR CARAWAN, *white, from eastern Tennessee*

MAY, *white, from eastern Kentucky. An almost unnoticeable limp.*

EMMA, *Tejana, from San Antonio, Texas*

NED, *white, from Atlanta, Georgia*

JOHN, *African-American, from Montgomery, Alabama. Very well dressed.*

Highlander Folk School
Monteagle, Tennessee
Spring, 1955

NOTES

This is a play about where we are, set in a time where we've been. If it feels like the present day keeps speaking up, let it.

All these actions actually happened. All the characters are inspired by actual people. But the timeline of events has been rearranged and telescoped and characters are amalgams of several different historical figures. A dramatic character is both more and less than a person; a character is not merely who a person was; it is also in some way what we take them to represent. Each of these characters must stand for many. Their actions are not literal, but figurative. There is no record of some of them having literally visited the Highlander Folk School. But, as Myles Horton often said, Highlander is an idea. Its influence has been felt at more removes from the South than this.

Or at no remove at all. In the midst of the writing and workshops for this play, Highlander, in its current existence as the Highlander Research and Education Center, was firebombed on March 29, 2018. There were no injuries; a main building was burned to the ground. White supremacists claimed responsibility. We were creating a play mirroring a history that all but literally repeated itself at the moment we were working.

All of which is a long way of saying: Inspired by True Events.

One became great by expecting the possible, another by expecting the eternal, but he who expected the impossible became greater than all.
Søren Kierkegaard

ACT ONE

DAY ONE

(Nine old wooden chairs in a circle. To the side, a tray of iced tea glasses and a phonograph. MRS CLARK is standing at a window, looking down a hill.)

(MR CARAWAN is tuning up his guitar.)

MR CARAWAN: What's he doing?

MRS CLARK: Just sitting in the police car. Pretending he's doing his paperwork.

MR CARAWAN: Can he see who's coming up the hill from where he is?

MRS CLARK: That's why he's there.

MR CARAWAN: But we got everybody up here already?

MRS CLARK: All but one.

(MAY enters and approaches MR CARAWAN.)

MAY: Morning.

MR CARAWAN: Hi.

MAY: Are you the teacher?

MR CARAWAN: We'll mostly be teaching each other.

MAY: Am I in the right place? I got invited to a school.

MR CARAWAN: This is a school.

MAY: I thought I'd be learning from experts. So who are the experts?

MR CARAWAN: If you got invited, one of the experts must be you.

MAY: Well, somebody's going to want their money back.

(EMMA *enters and heads straight for* MRS CLARK.)

EMMA: Who's in charge?

MRS CLARK: Well, really, you are.

EMMA: I am? Okay, then, I'm going to need to know a few things. What's the goal? Which people is this for? Who wants to stop us? How long have we got? Where are we now?

MRS CLARK: All of you are, I mean. In charge.

EMMA: Ah. Got it.

(NED *enters and heads for* MR CARAWAN.)

NED: When will we meet Mr Horton? I'll be proud to shake his hand. The Founding Father!

MR CARAWAN: Mr Horton spends most of his time on the road, raising money.

NED: It's important we talk, he and I. I'm Ned Edwards, from Atlanta.

MR CARAWAN: We don't expect him back until after this session is done.

NED: Well but then, he just…leaves the running of the place to…

MR CARAWAN: Mrs Clark is the new Education Director.

NED: Really. Well. When she shows up, you let me know. We should figure out what role you all want me to play this week. I'm something of a scholar of labor issues.

MR CARAWAN: That's very generous of you, but—

NED: But what I really want to know is, where do I get ahold of some of that famous Tennessee sippin' whiskey? My boss back in Atlanta expressly insisted that I not come back without a jug of that 'shine. Can you hook me up?

MR CARAWAN: This is a dry county.

NED: But my boss has been here, and he told me I should ask everybody about...

(JOHN *enters and takes in the scene.*)

NED: Crap.

(MRS CLARK *heads for* JOHN.)

MRS CLARK: Good morning.

JOHN: Did you know there'd be all these white people here?

MRS CLARK: It's all white people around here.

JOHN: I thought this was still the South, how can it be the South with only white people?

MRS CLARK: This is the mountains you're in now.

JOHN: There's white people in this meeting.

MRS CLARK: Mm hm.

JOHN: In Alabama, Black and white in the same meeting is against the law.

MRS CLARK: Here too.

JOHN: It is all very well for these well-meaning white folks to be breaking the law, maybe get put in jail for a bit, but you know it's different for you and me. Different scale of consequences.

MRS CLARK: I am aware. And I apologize if you were not told what to expect.

JOHN: What I'd been told was there were a lot of fine revolutionary women who come up here.

MR CARAWAN: *(Calling to* MRS CLARK*)* Mrs Clark?

JOHN: *Mrs* Clark. Crap.

MR CARAWAN: You want to start?

MRS CLARK: *(To* MR CARAWAN*)* Let's.

(In the natural course of things, all the white people are on one side of the room and the people of color are on the other. A moment)

MRS CLARK: Please sit.

(They do. There are several empty chairs.)

MRS CLARK: So first of all, you should know this is not officially happening.

EMMA: Why?

NED: Look around. This is illegal.

MRS CLARK: Highlander Folk School has been integrated since it opened over twenty years ago. But it is getting harder to gather like this.

NED: With all the unrest.

JOHN: With all the repression.

NED: The Supreme Court is moving faster than the country is ready for.

JOHN: We are ready. We are more than ready.

MRS CLARK: Airing our grievances with each other is not why we are here and not what this place is for.

(Beat)

MAY: Are we all the people there are going to be?

MRS CLARK: We had thought there would be more. But not everyone who wants to come here finds they can. Not everyone who sets out arrives here safely. I am glad you are with us. Feel free to introduce yourselves—

NED: I'm Ned Edwards from the C I O, which has supported this place for decades. Highlander has trained some of our finest organizers. I don't recognize any of you.

MRS CLARK: I suggest we use first names only. If word gets out to your home communities that you are here, there might be repercussions. We do get people here with agendas of their own.

JOHN: Spies?

MRS CLARK: It is not so simple. In some ways we are allies. In some ways we are not.

MR CARAWAN: One last caution: we are in Grundy County. This whole county, all this around here, is sundown counties.

NED: We don't have those in Georgia.

MR CARAWAN: You may have seen the signs at the county line—I will not say the word they use, but they warn Negroes not to let the sun set on them here.

EMMA: We have this in the West.

MAY: I didn't see any signs like that.

EMMA: They are not addressed to you.

JOHN: Am I the only one who had to arrive under cover of darkness? And take back roads in?

MR CARAWAN: Any Negro who has tried to live in this county has been driven out or killed. This isn't the Deep South, where they lynch to keep people down. Here they lynch to keep people out.

EMMA: But then why is Highlander here?

MRS CLARK: If you want to help people to change, you have to start from where they are. Our founders are from here. We have made our home here. We'll stay as long as we're allowed.

MR CARAWAN: Keep to the property. Don't stray from the buildings and paths after dark.

MRS CLARK: And welcome to Tennessee.

JOHN: What do we call *you*?

MRS CLARK: Call me Mrs Clark. Mr Carawan, would you lead us in song?

(MR CARAWAN *starts strumming his guitar.*)

MR CARAWAN: Here at Highlander, music is part of everything we do. We love it when you teach us the songs of your people, where you're from. Here's one we learned from a cotton mill worker from South Carolina, who learned it from her grandmother, who learned it during the time she was enslaved. Here it is the way she learned it. *(Singing:)*
I shall not, I shall not be moved
I shall not, I shall not be moved
Just like a tree, planted by the water
I shall not be moved
(Speaking) But when our friend from South Carolina had been here a few days, she said, I want to add a little something to my song, I want to change it, do you think I could, and she sung it like this. Join in:

(Singing, as the others tentatively join:)

MR CARAWAN & OTHERS:
We shall not, we shall not be moved
We shall not, we shall not be moved
Just like a tree, planted by the water
We shall not be moved
(Speaking) The song has traveled since then and it changes wherever it goes. *(Singing, with a nod to* MAY*:)*
The union is behind us, we shall not be moved
(The OTHERS join.)
The union is behind us, we shall not be moved
Just like a tree, planted by the water

We shall not be moved
(*Speaking*) Thank you. Let's do more of that soon. Mrs
Clark?

EMMA: Remind me to tell you a story about that song.

MR CARAWAN: You bet.

MRS CLARK: Thank you, Mr Carawan. Now let's try an
activity that—

NED: The usual procedure is to announce at the start
why we are meeting.

MAY: Hey, little mister. Who'd you say you were with
again?

NED: I'm with the C I O.

MAY: No, I've been with the C I O. The Congress of
Industrial Organizations, maybe you've heard of it, it's
a labor union. For working people. Which C I O are
you with?

NED: Same as you.

MAY: Your fingernails are mighty clean and shiny for a
working man.

NED: I ask again: why are we here?

MRS CLARK: I don't know. Why did you want to be
here?

EMMA: They told me this could be a way to get my
people what they need.

MRS CLARK: Then that's why you're here. Every so
often a person emerges with a natural genius for
leadership. We look for people like that.

MAY: So you want to know what our people need?

MRS CLARK: Each of you has some experience of
organizing or leading a movement, or somebody
thinks you could. There's a power of knowledge in
this room. If each of you knew what all of you knows,

and if you took that home… Who knows what could happen.

NED: You still haven't said why we were all invited here.

JOHN: You haven't said what *you* want.

(Beat)

MRS CLARK: Well then. Well then, you have been brought here because no one believes that a group of people like this can work together. I want to learn, from you, if we can. All right?

JOHN: All right.

MRS CLARK: Now let's try an activity.

NED: Is this like arts and crafts? Trace your hand and draw a turkey?

MRS CLARK: Thank you for volunteering.

NED: I wasn't.

MRS CLARK: But I knew you would. This is something you've all done. It goes by different names: the one-on-ones, house meetings, kitchen table, door knocking. As you know, this is the foundation of everything we do. Mr Carawan, would you be our prospect? Ned, knock on Mr Carawan's door and see if you can get him to join your organization.

NED: *(To MR CARAWAN)* Should I use my own organization?

MR CARAWAN: What organization are you with?

NED: The United Brotherhood of Carpenters and Joiners.

MR CARAWAN: In the C I O?

NED: That's right.

MAY: Nah. Tell the truth.

NED: I am.

MRS CLARK: Hold on. Let's assume Ned is telling the truth about who his people are.

MAY: Must be nice where you live.

NED: Atlanta.

MAY: Fancy. That explains it.

MRS CLARK: When you want to continue the exercise from your own experience, ask to step in.

MAY: Okay, I'm stepping in. You, Mr Carawan, is it?

MR CARAWAN: Call me Guy.

MAY: Guy, move on over.

NED: But you're a woman.

MAY: Thanks for noticing. I started work in hosiery mills when I was twelve years old. Go on, unionize me.

NED: Young lady, I'm here from the union that—

MAY: What's my name?

NED: I don't—forgive me, I don't—what is your name?

MAY: May.

NED: So, May, I'm from the union that—

MAY: What's your name?

NED: Do we really have to—

MAY: Would you rather draw a turkey?

NED: Good morning, Miss May, my name is Ned and I'm from the union. I've come to get you signed up today. Would now be a good time?

MAY: Hell no.

NED: Well. I know, nobody likes to start paying their union dues, but everybody in your shop is in the union or we can't represent you well.

MAY: You mean I can't work here if I'm not in your union?

NED: That's right. You see, otherwise the boss could just hire scabs, who'll work for next to nothing, in dangerous conditions.

MAY: Who would do that?

NED: Well. Negroes. Foreigners.

(Beat)

MAY: And hillbillies. Don't forget hillbillies.

(Beat)

NED: I'm just being honest.

MRS CLARK: We know. Thank you for sharing your community's truth.

EMMA: I'm stepping in.

NED: If we can't be honest with each other, what's the point?

MRS CLARK: True true.

EMMA: *(To MAY)* My turn. Stay there.

MAY: Go ahead.

EMMA: *Buenos días, señora*—and I would say your name because of course I know you already, I'm your neighbor—*Señora Maya, como estas, como esta su esposo, sus niños, y Tia Dolores como esta la mujer de mi prima del hermano de mi madre*—

MAY: Wait, what country is this in?

EMMA: This country. Well, *Tejas.* So first thing, I've got to ask her how her family is, each of them, by name, and then her extended family if she and I are related—

NED: What country are you from?

EMMA: This country.

MAY: What country am I supposed to be from?

EMMA: This country.

MAY: Then why are you talking that way?

EMMA: You should get across the Mississippi sometime.

NED: You mean the Rio Grande.

EMMA: I know what I mean. In two languages. Can I get back to talking with my friend here? *(To* MAY*)* So you've heard we're going to walk out. No more working for a few cents a day. Your family is ready, my family is ready, the neighborhood is ready. Are you ready?

MAY: I don't know if I'm ready.

EMMA: What do you need to make you ready?

MAY: What happens when the money runs out?

EMMA: We've been stockpiling food. We're sharing what we've got. It's not much but it should be enough. We'll get you what you need.

MAY: Will I have to walk a picket line?

EMMA: We'll all be there. But there's lots of other jobs.

MAY: What if I get arrested? What about my kids?

EMMA: We're organized. We go in shifts, anybody walking the line, their kids are with someone they know. What else?

MAY: Who's in charge of all this?

EMMA: You keep asking so many good questions, you're going to be in charge of some of it. So?

MAY: This really happened?

EMMA: *Claro que sí.*

MAY: That must have been something. That is not how it is for us.

MRS CLARK: John, step in?

JOHN: No, this is a scene about labor unions. Labor unions do not admit Negroes. Please go on. I am learning a lot.

MAY: I'll step in. Guy, take my place. *(To* EMMA*)* I didn't get your name.

EMMA: Emma.

MAY: Emma, you get in there, too. You're husband and wife, let's skip the introductions.

(MR CARAWAN *and* EMMA *sit as a couple with* MAY *as their guest.)*

MAY: I've knocked on a lot of doors. I'm not going to lie to you. No one wants to go first.

MR CARAWAN: Like who?

MAY: I'm not naming their names, the same as I won't name yours. But you are not alone in hurting. Other families have kids sick and dying. Family down this creek just lost a boy. Carter's boy, Henry. Company doctor said he was sick but I heard the story and, no, he starved to death. He's not the only one.

EMMA: *(Breaking character)* Wait. What?

JOHN: Starved to death?

MAY: People. Welcome to the mountains.

(Beat)

JOHN: Lord have mercy.

MAY: Not here to complain, here to work. *(To* MR CARAWAN*)* Talk with some of your neighbors, that's all I'm asking. Hear what each other have to say.

EMMA: But what can people like us do?

MAY: That's not my place to tell you.

NED: Question.

MAY: Shoot.

NED: They're called one-on-ones. Why's the wife there?

MAY: The wives like it better if I'm not meeting alone with their men. And two, she's the one going to do most of the work. But he needs to believe it's his idea. She needs him to buy into it or she won't feel right about doing it.

EMMA: So she needs his permission?

MAY: Best if they need each other's permission. They both need to see the good it does their family if they do this work, take these risks. That way it's an act of love. That'll matter down the line.

MRS CLARK: Go on.

MR CARAWAN: You want us to go make trouble.

MAY: No sir.

MR CARAWAN: You want them to throw us all out of our homes. They own everything.

MAY: If they can do that, is this a home? When some men can just come tell you to clear out of it? And they have a stack of papers and they each have a gun, and not a good man's hunting rifle he uses to feed his family. Army guns. But they won't be in uniform.

MR CARAWAN: How'd you know all that?

MAY: Because that's what they did to my people. We got no place anymore, not even a place like this. My people never knew what hit them. But we know now. And we were just like you.

MR CARAWAN: Is this about a union? We got a union. Union's no help if there's no jobs. The machines now do the work of ten men, twenty. They don't need us anymore. Everybody's on relief, but—

MAY: Good men are leaving so their wives can go
on relief. But the company owns the county so the
company says who gets relief. There's nowhere to turn.

EMMA: We've got to do something.

MAY: I think you're right.

MR CARAWAN: Preacher's been warning us people like
you might come.

MAY: Somebody pays that preacher's salary, though.

EMMA: They do. And the sheriffs and the deputies,
they pay them too.

MAY: You're right again.

MR CARAWAN: So why don't you just say what we
should do?

MAY: No, no. When I leave here, remember two things.
I never said make trouble. You said make trouble. I
never said "county" or "company." You said county
and company. You had those ideas. You got them from
somewhere, from your neighbors or your own good
sense.

MR CARAWAN: Our preacher warned us about ideas
like that.

MAY: Then the joke's on him, because when he was
trying to scare you, he got you thinking instead. You're
smarter than he thinks you are. We are smarter than
everybody thinks we are. When we put our heads
together.

MR CARAWAN: You know what'll happen to me if they
find out?

MAY: You could be blacklisted. I'm not lying to you.

EMMA: You're the first one who isn't.

MAY: I know speaking up is absolutely the last thing
you want to do. But a man who's lost about all he had,

as soon as he takes this step his life starts up joyful again.

EMMA: When is that meeting?

MAY: How soon can you organize it?

(Beat)

MR CARAWAN: Why me?

MAY: I've asked around, and your name keeps coming up. Your neighbors think well of you.

MR CARAWAN: Don't know why.

EMMA: I know why.

MAY: They need leaders.

MR CARAWAN: We've got bosses aplenty.

EMMA: Nothing like the same as you.

MAY: *(To the group)* Yes! That is why you want the woman in the room! Woman like that is worth ten times what I can do. *(To EMMA)* Who else should be there?

EMMA: We're not going to give you names either.

MAY: Good. That's good instincts. You don't know me. But you know them. Would you ask them yourselves?

EMMA: How many?

MAY: No more than a handful. Quieter that way. It'll be an organizing committee. It needs you on it.

EMMA: Honey? What do you think?

MR CARAWAN: Yeah. Okay. Lord oh Lord.

EMMA: Will you be there?

MAY: You don't need me.

MR CARAWAN: You going to run off and make trouble somewhere else?

MAY: The owners and the county know I'm here. They always know when there's someone new around. So far they think I'm just a poor miner's wife trying to find where her husband ran off to. They had a good laugh and let me go. But if they hear people making up stories about how I came into their houses making trouble, they will come in a car and drag me in and I will not be seen again.

EMMA: How do you know that?

MAY: Because that's what happened to my brothers. They said they ran them out of town. But come spring their bones were found three miles downstream. Don't do that to me. You are going to do this thing yourselves. *(To the group)* And they did. So, yeah. That's kind of how I done it.

EMMA: So where was this? What happened?

MRS CLARK: And what is the problem in your home community you're looking to work on?

MAY: That was in Kentucky. Leslie County, Harlan County.

MR CARAWAN: Harlan County, Kentucky?

NED: I think I've heard of you. That was you?

MAY: No, it was them. It was them.

EMMA: What happened?

MAY: Long story. The man I was thinking of there, that man died, they killed him. Beat him to death. Nobody ever said who. So we knew. His wife and kids, they had to get out. I don't know where she is now. So my problem in my home community, which I don't know where that is because I'm blacklisted in Kentucky, my problem is when I organize a person they get killed.

EMMA: *Oyé*, that is not your fault.

MAY: I know whose fault it is, and if I could get to them I would kill them, but I can't. So that's two problems I've got.

(NED *stands.*)

NED: Forgive me, if I…I did not understand who you were. You all don't—Harlan County. How do they not know?

MR CARAWAN: I know a little. I thought that war ended a long time ago.

MAY: It never ended.

NED: Harlan County was a great uprising of American working people.

MAY: We lost. No one wants to remember.

NED: Some of us do.

MRS CLARK: Thank you. Let's take a break.

(*As they disperse,* MRS CLARK *to* JOHN:)

MRS CLARK: Let's you and I have a talk.

JOHN: All right, let's.

(JOHN *and* MRS CLARK *cross away.*)

MAY: Thanks for helping me do that. It's been a long time. You both did good.

NED: You said you were blacklisted.

MAY: I've been scuffling for a while. No one can hire me. Even as a volunteer I'm poison, I'd get any group blacklisted just for knowing me. Red-baited. Assembly line work and organizing is all I've ever done. And my children, but that's…I do miss knocking on the doors. There is so much to be done and I won't be let to do any. If I could just come in early and set up the chairs.

(*Across the room:*)

MRS CLARK: You do understand that I am in charge here.

JOHN: I thought we were all in charge.

MRS CLARK: I'm in charge of making sure you all feel like you're in charge.

JOHN: Why would they ask you to do that?

MRS CLARK: Mr Myles Horton is that very rare man who knows how to get out of the way. This is a vehicle. They left me the keys.

JOHN: Why?

MRS CLARK: To see if I could do it. And now who is standing in my way? Not some white man.

JOHN: I'm not standing in your way.

MRS CLARK: We are here to see if we can learn from each other. And here's you, refusing to be seen to learn anything from anyone.

JOHN: Oh so I'm your problem? Not Mister Charlie over there?

MRS CLARK: There's him and there's you and so that's two problems I've got.

JOHN: Come on, don't be this way to me.

MRS CLARK: Don't what now? Don't you say don't to me—

JOHN: Why are you being this way? You're not talking to anybody else like this—

MRS CLARK: Because you matter.

JOHN: I thought everybody matters to you the same.

MRS CLARK: If I was Jesus. But given that I'm not Jesus, and given how little we matter to everybody else, I'm going to make sure you know you matter to me. I can

tell you've got people where you're from who let you
know you matter.

JOHN: You are not my mama.

MRS CLARK: Oh, I have a thing or two to say to your
mama.

JOHN: I've got nothing to prove to these people.

MRS CLARK: That's right. You are here to get
knowledge and carry it home. Take what Mister
Charlie has so he won't even know it's gone.

JOHN: What do you want from me?

MRS CLARK: Participate. Try to learn, and if you can't
learn, try to teach.

(Across the room:)

NED: I'm from district headquarters in Atlanta. This
school has had a long-standing relationship with our
union. Training our organizers. We at the C I O have
sent a whole lot of money this way.

MR CARAWAN: True, true.

NED: But you also have a reputation as a bunch of
radicals.

MR CARAWAN: We were founded to do Christian good
works.

MAY: You mean because they're integrated? C I O has
always been integrated.

MR CARAWAN: Somewhat integrated.

MAY: At least it's not the AFL. They're as segregated as
an Alabama bus station.

NED: The C I O is merging with the A F L.

MAY: Son of a bitch. I'd heard it and didn't want to
believe it.

(The two sides rejoin.)

NED: And before we do, we're going to have to clean house. The C I O is lousy with reds. That was maybe okay in the '30s, with the Depression, people were desperate, anybody can make a mistake.

MRS CLARK: Why are you here?

NED: Some people would be just as happy to shut you down outright. Some of us think you deserve a last chance to defend yourselves. Like I said: I'm here to learn. Why are you here, Mrs Clark?

MRS CLARK: I taught elementary school, until shortly ago. I taught children to read.

NED: Why until shortly ago?

MRS CLARK: The school board learned that I was teaching the children to read the State Constitution.

NED: Why would you do that?

MRS CLARK: So they would know what it says.

JOHN: And they fired you for that?

MRS CLARK: No, they did not fire me for that.

NED: But they did fire you? What for?

MRS CLARK: They fired me because I was a member of the N A A C P.

MAY: I don't know what that is.

MRS CLARK: The National Association for the Advancement of Colored People.

NED: An illegal, anti-American, communist organization.

JOHN: A patriotic organization helping Americans to advance.

NED: Then why is it illegal?

JOHN: I don't know. Why is it legal to be a member of the Ku Klux Klan?

Mrs Clark: And that is more than enough about
me! We have many more important subjects to cover.
Please sit.

(As they do:)

Mrs Clark: In your house meetings, when your
people talk about making trouble, speaking up, what
are they thinking of?

May: They're afraid. They're afraid to follow the
rules for filing a complaint with the county—afraid of
reprisals, afraid they won't be able to fill out the forms
right. A lot of them don't have more than a fourth
grade education and that's rusty.

John: That's...

May: What? That's a surprise to you?

John: Where I'm from, the white school is so much
more inviting than ours. I would have thought it
would be a pleasure to go to school, for a white child.

May: Where I'm from, there aren't any colored, so the
white school is the colored school. We're all the poor
people there are. And the company pays almost no
taxes and they own almost everything. We don't have
much.

Mrs Clark: Hold on. You'll hear me say that
sometimes when I want us to come back to something
but we're getting off track. We can argue over who has
it hardest, or we can talk about what our people can
do.

(Beat)

May: When there's enough of them, and they feel
ready, the county commissioners are supposed to have
a meeting every month, and my people will go, as a
group.

MRS CLARK: Good. Public hearings are one of the best tools we have. Let's see that. Who can be a county commissioner?

EMMA: I know that guy. I'll be him.

(EMMA *and the others arrange themselves.*)

MRS CLARK: And who has a problem from home they want their people—we're your people—that you want us to present when they take questions? Something specific.

JOHN: I've got one. I hear this a lot.

EMMA: *(Doing an old white man impression)* We have just a couple of minutes to entertain questions from the floor. Yes, you, there, in the back.

JOHN: Why is the road to my house a dirt road?

EMMA: Boy, you know there's only so much money.

JOHN: Boy? Really.

EMMA: *(Dropping out of character)* It's not me, it's this guy, he's an asshole. Pardon me.

JOHN: The roads to the white ladies' houses are paved.

MAY: Hey, the road to my house isn't paved.

JOHN: Now isn't that out of order, isn't she out of order—

MRS CLARK: Hold on. That right there. You have a choice.

(Beat)

JOHN: Yes, why isn't the road to *her* house paved either?

EMMA: People, there's not enough money to pave all the roads.

JOHN: I pay taxes. Do you pay taxes?

EMMA: I surely do.

JOHN: So how can the county afford to pave the road to your house fresh every couple years, and mine and hers never at all?

MAY: It's not fair!

EMMA: Little lady—

MAY: Little lady?

EMMA: *(Out of character)* It's this guy, I'm telling you, such a pig.

MRS CLARK: Hold on.

MAY: Why? It's true, it's not fair.

MRS CLARK: I know, but think about it.

MAY: He knows it's unfair. He doesn't care.

MRS CLARK: So what doesn't he know? Teach him.

JOHN: Sir. We know you believe that we and our children are dirty and never on time.

EMMA: Facts are facts.

JOHN: But did you know that the reason our people are so often late to work and our children are late to school is unforeseen delays due to road conditions?

MRS CLARK: There you go.

JOHN: And when we go downtown, and your store people and the white ladies—

MRS CLARK: Hold on.

JOHN: Come on! The *ladies* whose houses we clean complain that we're dirty—

MAY: We track dirt everywhere.

MR CARAWAN: They think we're dirty people—

JOHN: But it is nothing about us. It is that road.

MAY: He's right. That road makes us dirty.

MR CARAWAN: And our cars.

MAY: And our children.

JOHN, MAY & MR CARAWAN: Pave our roads! Pave our roads! Pave our roads!

MRS CLARK: Hold on.

JOHN: Why?

MRS CLARK: Because that's good. Now, back to him.

JOHN: We shop in your stores, we work in your businesses, we go to your schools.

MAY: A lot of the time and money they spend cleaning is for cleaning up after your dirt road.

JOHN, MAY & MR CARAWAN: Pave our roads! Pave our roads! Pave our roads!

MRS CLARK: Hold on. So what's your big point?

JOHN: The county will save money by paving the road to her house.

MAY: And his house. And his house.

JOHN, MAY, MR CARAWAN & NED: Pave our roads! Pave our roads! Pave our roads!

EMMA: Ladies and gentlemen, you make an interesting point. We will form a committee and they will make a report.

MAY: Crap.

NED: You do know that guy.

JOHN: What does that even mean?

MAY: It means they don't believe us, they'll only believe someone who brings numbers and looks like them.

MRS CLARK: So what now?

NED: Who will be on the committee?

JOHN: When will the report be done?

EMMA: And that's all the time we have this month—

MAY: Crap!

EMMA: We will take this up next month as New Business.

JOHN: But this will take months.

MRS CLARK: Oh, years. How many years has your road been dirt?

MAY: Since the beginning of time.

EMMA: *(Dropping her character for good)* And it will stay that way to the end of time and the hearse that drives your great grandchildren to the graveyard will have mud on the fenders. As long as you follow the rules.

JOHN: So we what? Break the rules?

NED: Make a nuisance of ourselves?

MRS CLARK: Maybe, but why?

MAY: Piss 'em off.

MRS CLARK: Okay. The main point of all this is what?

EMMA: It has to be about them. Everything always has to be about them. How they want things around them to be. How they want their country to be.

MRS CLARK: Okay, and?

EMMA: What you all said before. They want their places all the time clean. So before the next county meeting, in their clean county meeting hall, you all walk there, on that muddy dirt road, and you walk that road right into their meeting.

JOHN: Make a mess?

EMMA: Stage a demonstration. Do you know what a demonstration is?

MAY: Marching.

NED: Signs.

MR CARAWAN: Chanting.

MRS CLARK: Yes all that and why?

EMMA: A demonstration is teaching someone
something by showing them how it works. A march is
for when they think they have the people on their side.
So you show you have the people on *your* side. People
who care enough to make a spectacle of themselves.
Sometimes you have to make a spectacle of yourself.

MRS CLARK: Let's take a break.

(MR CARAWAN *brings out the tray of iced tea glasses.*)

(EMMA *grabs a couple of glasses.*)

(MRS CLARK *stares out the window and down.*)

(EMMA, *carrying two glasses, approaches* MAY.)

(NED, *drinking tea, strolls to the window where* MRS
CLARK *stands.*)

NED: Is there someone out there?

MRS CLARK: He seems to be gone for the day.

(MR CARAWAN, *carrying two glasses, crosses to* MRS
CLARK.)

MR CARAWAN: Would you care for some tea, Mrs
Clark?

MRS CLARK: That is most kind of you, yes I would.

(MR CARAWAN *gives* MRS CLARK *a glass. She drinks.* NED
watches. MR CARAWAN *looks at him.* NED *turns to the
window.*)

NED: Beautiful evening coming on.

EMMA: *Té?*

MAY: Thank you.

MRS CLARK: Supper soon.

NED: And where do we eat?

MRS CLARK: All together.

(NED *can't help but turn to* MRS CLARK *in shock. She is not surprised.*)

(EMMA *and* MAY *sip tea.*)

MAY: I heard someone is cooking the supper for us. Did you hear that?

EMMA: I did.

MAY: I won't know what to do with myself.

(EMMA *and* MAY *fall silent.* JOHN *strolls over to* EMMA.)

JOHN: Interesting place.

EMMA: Yeah, I'm not sure about it either.

JOHN: This your first time in Tennessee?

EMMA: That's right. I've picked apples in Ohio and chopped cotton in Alabama. If there's farms I'll probably work here too someday.

JOHN: You've chopped cotton.

EMMA: Sure, haven't you?

JOHN: I am a minister's son and a graduate of Morehouse College. I have never chopped cotton.

EMMA: Chopped cotton, tied carrots, hoed lettuce, harvested hops.

JOHN: And you're an organizer.

EMMA: I keep trying. I heard you say your people can't get into these unions.

JOHN: That's right.

EMMA: My people too. So we made our own union. Just a thought.

JOHN: My people who do that sort of thing are killed by the Klan.

EMMA: The Klan lynches my people, too. And we are kept from voting. And we are denied good schools. And we are not allowed to buy good homes.

JOHN: So you're saying I should get over it.

EMMA: I am saying we have problems in common.

(MR CARAWAN's guitar is noticeable.)

JOHN: One of my problems is all this singing.

EMMA: Can't you sing?

JOHN: Not a note.

EMMA: You don't sing and you don't chop cotton.

JOHN: I listen to modern jazz and I would be living in Paris if there weren't so much to do here.

EMMA: I bet you can't dance, either.

JOHN: I can dance.

EMMA: I just hope they don't make us do any of that square dancing. I know we're in white people country but come on.

(MAY, who has been watching EMMA intently, blinks and turns away. MR CARAWAN strolls over.)

MR CARAWAN: May I interrupt? You promised a story about that song.

EMMA: I did.

MR CARAWAN: Please tell the story, do, please?

MRS CLARK: Is this about the song?

EMMA: Yeah. So I was in jail one time, in Tejas.

MAY: What were you charged with?

EMMA: Creating a public disturbance. I think. I've been arrested a lot. Just being me.

MAY: What did you do?

EMMA: I got born in West San Antonio, that's what I did. *Mi abuelo,* my grandfather, would take me to hear the speeches on *la Plaza.* Old Mexican Revolutionaries, Communists, anarchists. I started talking with people— *(To* MAY*)* House meetings, like you. They all said the same thing: no jobs, no food, not for us. Women were shelling pecans in tin sheds for a few cents a day. One day I stood up in *la Plaza* and I started speaking. One day those women walked off the job. The bossmen said, who's your leader, and they said, Her.

NED: Wait. The San Antonio Pecan Strike, that's a famous strike, we study that strike, that was one of the biggest locals in the country, ten thousand women. You led that? But that was years ago.

EMMA: I was nineteen years old.

NED: I know who you are, you're—

EMMA: Yeah, I don't use that name anymore. Okay?

MAY: Tell the story.

EMMA: I was nineteen and crazy and I had a big mouth. They arrested everybody, sprayed us with hoses, put so many in a cell we couldn't lie down. They'd let me out every couple of days to negotiate to end the strike.

MAY: How long did this go on?

EMMA: Weeks and weeks. Our spirits got pretty low. But the C I O—

(Glasses are raised.)

EMMA: The C I O sent a couple of guys to see what the hell was happening. They got arrested too. And one night in the jail, from over on the other side, the men's side, I hear *(Singing quietly)*
No no no, no nos moveran
No no no, no nos moveran

MR CARAWAN: The same song!

EMMA: Those two guys, they'd been here, to
Highlander, and one of them spoke Spanish, he was
translating, and they were singing all those songs, all
the men were singing, to cheer us up, telling us they
wanted us to win. That's how I heard about this place.
True story. I thought, Tennessee, damn, that must be
the land of freedom and beautiful, beautiful men.

MAY: What happened with the strike?

EMMA: We won. So the next year they replaced
everybody with machines. Texas Rangers said they
couldn't protect me from the Ku Klux Klan and I had
to get out of *Tejas* and why didn't I go back where I
came from? I said, I'm from here. Those guys—you
guys—you keep forgetting that there was a fight, here,
before your fight. Comanches and Conquistadores
made war for centuries and when the dust settled what
was left, here, was me. Saying stuff like that'll get you
kicked out of *Tejas* right there.

MAY: And you've been roaming since then.

EMMA: That's how it is, somebody's always kicking
somebody's ass out of *Tejas*. I'll get back there
someday.

MAY: Why?

EMMA: Ah, you know, it's home.

(Dinner bell rings.)

MRS CLARK: Supper is served.

MAY: *(To EMMA)* Could I eat with you? If I could just—
could I sit with you at supper?

EMMA: Come on.

*(Everyone goes but MRS CLARK and NED, who hesitates to
go with the others. MRS CLARK sees, and waits.)*

NED: Mrs Clark. You must know the National Association for the Advancement of Colored People is a Communist organization.

MRS CLARK: Truly I do not.

NED: The government of my state says it is.

MRS CLARK: So does the government of mine. That does not make it true.

NED: It makes it the law. You taught Negro children to read the State Constitution. Why?

MRS CLARK: In South Carolina, if a Negro wants to register to vote, they have to pass a test to prove they know the State Constitution backwards and forwards. One might almost think that test was designed to make it nearly impossible for a person to vote.

NED: But what does all this prepare them for? What sort of jobs can they get?

MRS CLARK: The boys, mostly manual labor; the girls, domestic service. Mechanics and maids. A few, the very intelligent ones, may be allowed to teach school.

NED: My point exactly. What are you educating them to do?

MRS CLARK: They are to advance.

NED: Mrs Clark, the C I O is doing its best to prove that it is not a Communist organization. Now the new Education Director of our training school is a member of a Communist organization.

MRS CLARK: Rest assured I am not.

NED: You were not fully informed. You could quit them and I would say no more. We could maintain our association and you could keep your job here. Anyone can make a mistake.

MRS CLARK: Mr Edwards, are you a member of the Klan?

NED: What did you say?

MRS CLARK: I asked if you were a member of the Ku Klux Klan.

NED: What makes you think that about me? Because I'm white? Because I'm a white man I must be in the Klan?

MRS CLARK: If you were, you would not be our first Klansman. And anyone can make a mistake.

NED: I'm a good union man. Our people say they learn things here, some of them helpful things. I came to see for myself. That's the reason I'm here. Do you want me to leave? And make my report as of now?

MRS CLARK: I hope you will stay, and when you go home I hope you will be truthful.

NED: You ask a lot.

MRS CLARK: True, true.

NIGHT

(*Starlight.* MAY *sits, not relaxed.* EMMA *enters behind her.*)

EMMA: Are you okay?

MAY: Trouble sleeping in there. Sorry if I woke you.

EMMA: You didn't. I'm used to sleeping any old where, but...

MAY: Me too, but...

EMMA: Keep you company?

MAY: Feel free. If I'd known we were both awake we could have talked in there.

EMMA: Me and my sisters, for hours.

MAY: Me too. At least here we don't have to pile into bed together.

EMMA: Yeah... I miss it, sometimes.

MAY: Did you tell stories?

EMMA: Stories, gossip, songs.

MAY: This was in San Antonio?

EMMA: Yeah.

MAY: Where will you go after this?

EMMA: I don't know. You?

MAY: I don't know.

(Beat)

EMMA: Could you sleep now?

MAY: Not yet.

EMMA: Me neither.

MAY: Why, I wonder.

EMMA: Something on our minds.

MAY: I was lying there thinking.

EMMA: Me too.

MAY: What about?

EMMA: You.

MAY: That's funny.

EMMA: Right?

MAY: I was lying there thinking I wonder what she's lying there thinking about.

EMMA: I was thinking about being back home sleeping all piled in together with my sisters and here you and I were but in different beds so far away.

MAY: Isn't that strange.

EMMA: I've shared my bed with women before.

MAY: Your sisters.

(NED *enters from elsewhere, in undershirt and suit pants, startled to find* MAY *and* EMMA *there.)*

NED: Hey. Evening. I don't suppose you gals have such a thing as a drink on you? If I could just get a sip of that—I was told I could get some of that Tennessee moonshine—

MAY: It's a dry county.

NED: This is the craziest place I have been to in my life. When I go to bed at home I've had a drink or three, and I am lying next to my wife who loves me. Here I can't buy a drink at all and I'm sharing a room with a Negro man who would happily slit my throat. Evening.

EMMA: You must have bunked with men before.

NED: In the service, the barracks had all sorts. But not his sort.

MAY: What are you going to do?

NED: I will not be put out of my sleeping quarters by him. I am waiting until he is sound asleep. But I could surely use a drink of liquor. You got the same problem?

MAY: Yeah, we can't sleep either. Oh.

NED: What?

EMMA: What?

MAY: Nothing. I just figured something out.

NED: I've been sitting in bed smoking all my cigarettes. I can't tell if he's asleep or not. *(Beat)* Don't let me interrupt.

EMMA: What were we saying?

MAY: I think we were saying people can be a comfort to each other.

EMMA: There is a solace in friendship that I wish I had sometimes.

MAY: Yes.

NED: Nah, this doesn't work either, I've had it, I'm going back in there. Can't get over it, I can usually sleep just fine. Crazy place.

MAY: Good night.

(NED *goes. A silence*)

MAY: Sometimes when you are knocking on doors, the people who open the door will be…A pair of women will invite you in. Sisters, maiden sisters. Or friends. Dear friends. I guess people find all kinds of ways to keep house. Why are you smiling? What's funny?

EMMA: I'm funny. Sometimes I picture things that are so ridiculous.

MAY: Like what?

EMMA: Why are you smiling?

MAY: I don't know. Because you are. What are you picturing that's so ridiculous?

EMMA: Knock knock.

MAY: Who's there?

EMMA: Good morning, ma'am.

MAY: Good morning, ma'am, who?

EMMA: I am going door to door this morning, speaking to our neighbors.

MAY: Well, how do you do? (*She sticks her hand out.*)

(EMMA *takes* MAY'*s hand.*)

MAY: Whenever I hear that, "going door to door," I picture two doors meeting each other.

EMMA: Now that's funny.

MAY: And they both open, you know? Each of them is a way for the other to enter someplace new.

EMMA: It is a pleasure to meet you.

MAY: It is a pleasure to meet you. Would you like to come in?

EMMA: I would like that very much.

MAY: I think I might be ready to go back to my bed.

EMMA: I think I might be ready for that too.

DAY TWO

(Morning light. Some of a song from the guitar as people settle in. MRS CLARK is watching out the window again.)

MR CARAWAN: ...and save some energy if you can today, because tonight there will be square dancing.

(JOHN moans quietly.)

MR CARAWAN: ...And that is always a highlight of our workshops at Highlander.

(EMMA and MAY enter together, a bit rushed, and take their seats.)

MRS CLARK: Good morning. I trust everyone slept well.

(NED moans quietly. EMMA and MAY think inexpressible thoughts.)

MRS CLARK: Mr Carawan, will you lead us in song?

MR CARAWAN: Does anyone have a song to share from where they're from? Anyone?

MAY: I know one. This is from Kentucky. *(Singing)*
Come all of you good workers,
Good news to you I'll tell,
Of how the good old union
Has come in here to dwell.

MAY & MR CARAWAN:
Which side are you on?
Which side are you on?

MAY:
We've started our good battle,
We know we're sure to win,
Because we've got the gun thugs
A-lookin' very thin.

ALL:
Which side are you on?
Which side are you on?

MAY:
If you go up to Harlan County
There is no neutral there,
You'll either be a union man
Or a thug for J H Blair

ALL:
Which side are you on?
Which side are you on?
Which side are you on?
Which side are you on?

MRS CLARK: Thank you. So today.

JOHN: Could I—there was something from yesterday,
and it kept me up a lot of the night—

MRS CLARK: Please.

JOHN: That whole public meeting scenario implies that
these representatives—

EMMA: This guy.

JOHN: If this guy fails to exercise the will of the people,
he might lose their votes. Yes? And be out of a job.

EMMA: But I love my job!

JOHN: But almost none of my people can vote. All those appurtenances of a functioning democracy, that's just not where we live.

NED: But—if that were true—I mean, look at you. You've done well.

JOHN: I have. It took work.

NED: But that's great, that's what you want, right? Back when I was a boy, there weren't any colored folks like you.

JOHN: There were a few.

NED: I'm just saying, it seems like you already won.

JOHN: Won what?

NED: You've come up in the world. Guys like me are trying to stay in the same place. Just a matter of time before I come down.

JOHN: That's nothing to do with me.

NED: You people have made progress.

JOHN: A few of us. We are the exception. I did some things that got me noticed, opportunities came my way and I'm working to take advantage.

NED: But see, opportunities got created for you. Nobody created any opportunities for us.

JOHN: Yes they did. Of course they did. I can see them very well.

NED: Well, I don't I guess.

MRS CLARK: Hold on. *(To* JOHN*)* You brought up a problem. A sense that there's no democracy for your people. But remember earlier in the day? *(To* MAY*)* What did your people feel?

MAY: They're not in a democracy either. They've got no say.

MRS CLARK: What could his people do? What have other people done?

JOHN: *(To* MAY *and* EMMA*)* I would think what you two did—the house meetings. Tell them they need to take action, they need to register, they need to vote.

MRS CLARK: Let's start with that today. Who wants to be told they should register to vote? Anyone? That's fine, I'll do it myself. *(And she becomes a much older woman, her own South Carolina accent getting stronger)* Well now, well now, young man, nice to meet you, nice to meet you—

JOHN: Thank you, ma'am. I wanted to talk to you today about—

MRS CLARK: Well that's grand, let's have a talk, you come on in here, let's be comfortable—

JOHN: I don't want to take up too much of your time, I wanted to discuss—

MRS CLARK: Now you look hungry, don't you look hungry, can I—

JOHN: I'm fine, really—

MRS CLARK: Can I offer you something?

JOHN: Really, there's no—

MRS CLARK: Now let me see what I've got in the ice box, wish I had some ice, I'll tell you that—

JOHN: Hold, could we hold—

MRS CLARK: But let me see now, let me see, won't take a minute—

JOHN: Hold? Could we—didn't you yesterday—hold on?

MR CARAWAN: Mrs Clark, have mercy on him.

MRS CLARK: All right, all right, I was going to go in the kitchen and make him a batch of biscuits if he'd let me.

JOHN: What just happened?

MAY: You're a guest in her home.

EMMA: You're beginning a relationship.

MR CARAWAN: You're about to ask her to do something new and dangerous. She is frightened. Let her show you something she already knows how to do.

JOHN: So this is not like canvassing door to door in the city, or pastoral visits to my father's congregation.

MR CARAWAN: This is new for you too. Take your time. You're asking her to change. Start by meeting her where she is.

MRS CLARK: Can we get back to my old country gal? I'm loving her.

JOHN: Please.

MRS CLARK: All right. All right now.

JOHN: So as I was—

MRS CLARK: Did you like your biscuits?

JOHN: I...I did, yes. They were delicious.

MRS CLARK: No, no, not my best, not my best, I made a much better batch just the other day, now what day was that, it wasn't Sunday, didn't take breakfast Sunday, up early cooking for church supper, and it wasn't—was it Monday? It may have been Monday—

JOHN: What made that batch better than this batch? I can't imagine them being much better than this.

MRS CLARK: Well, you'll just have to come back another day and I'll show you.

JOHN: That would be grand. So I expect you're wondering what brings me here today.

MRS CLARK: Is it Bibles?

JOHN: I'm sorry?

MRS CLARK: Are you selling Bibles? We do get young men like yourself come through from time to time—

JOHN: No, not Bibles.

MRS CLARK: Well, good, because you'd be wasting your time, I've got a Bible, it is my prop and my support, don't you feel that, too?

JOHN: I do, but no. Why I'm here today—

MAY: Hold on.

JOHN: Yes! I do, ma'am. "The Lord is a refuge for the oppressed, a refuge in times of trouble."

MRS CLARK: Amen. Bless His name. That's from the Psalms, isn't it?

JOHN: It is.

MRS CLARK: I do love the Psalms.

JOHN: Yes, ma'am. We both know our Bible, that's not what I'm here about today.

MRS CLARK: Well, I've been waiting for you to tell me what you are here about.

JOHN: Well, I—

MRS CLARK: Just waiting patiently all this time.

JOHN: You know, those words, "times of trouble," it's as if they were sent to me just now, for a purpose. These are times of trouble, aren't they?

MRS CLARK: True, true.

JOHN: The Lord calls us to Him as a refuge. But He also calls us to each other, doesn't He? The Lord helps them who help themselves, isn't that so?

MRS CLARK: That is a mighty fine suit.

JOHN: I'm—what?

MRS CLARK: That suit, it is mighty fine. You look mighty fine in it.

JOHN: Thank you?

MRS CLARK: Now why are you dressed like that, and it's not even a Sunday?

JOHN: I am leading by example.

MRS CLARK: Now what does that mean?

JOHN: I am—so many of our people, we dress and carry ourselves so as not to be noticed, not to be threatening, not to show anyone up. We are disguising ourselves as, as failures, and we're not.

MRS CLARK: Why do you talk that way?

JOHN: I hope to show by how I dress and how I speak that a Black man can succeed at the highest level not by playing sports or gambling or selling Jesus or getting that government job, but with his intelligence, his education—

MRS CLARK: You're very flashy.

JOHN: Not flash. Quality. I'm a graduate of Morehouse College, and—

MRS CLARK: Undergrad?

JOHN: I'm…yes, undergraduate.

MRS CLARK: So you've got a Bachelor's degree?

JOHN: Yes, yes, I do, I graduated—

MRS CLARK: Got your Master's?

JOHN: No, not yet, no, I'm taking some time to assess my—

MRS CLARK: Now, me, I did some of my undergraduate work at Columbia University, up there in New York City, and then I did some at Atlanta University in Georgia, but my degree is from Benedict College here in South Carolina. That's my Bachelor's degree. Now my Master's is from Hampton, up in Virginia—people shall I let him get up now?

EMMA: Let him up!

MR CARAWAN: Have mercy on him!

JOHN: I do not know what just happened.

MAY: She got you talking about yourself.

EMMA: And it seems like that's your favorite subject.

JOHN: What am I not doing?

MAY: Listening.

JOHN: But I—she—

MAY: You're not listening now.

MRS CLARK: Let's try one more time. Tell me what you want.

JOHN: I am hoping that you will register to vote.

MRS CLARK: Why?

JOHN: Why?

MRS CLARK: Why? What's in it for me?

JOHN: A chance for a fair share of the resources of this area. Representation. Justice.

MRS CLARK: What's in it for me I mean except getting my house firebombed by gun thugs and my face spit in by courthouse layabouts, my husband and me losing our jobs, our children expelled from school, probably having to leave our home, never to return, or face almost certain ruin and death. Even having you in my house is an act of great courage. Do you understand that? These are small towns. Everything is seen and known. And even in the face of all that, if this woman tries to register, she will face eligibility tests and poll taxes and the likelihood that even if she gets through all that and is registered and lives until election day, her ballot will be thrown away, with laughter, by monstrous men. So tell me what I am voting for. You will need to know.

JOHN: You mentioned children. Do you have children?

MRS CLARK: Yes.

JOHN: They are why. Even if all that happens, your children will see you try. They will see you have hope that things will be better. For them. We fail, if we fail, so that they might succeed. Please, ma'am, please. Register and vote.

MRS CLARK: Well now. I might vote for you.

JOHN: Oh. Me but I'm—

MRS CLARK: That's why you're asking me for my vote, isn't it? Because you're running for office?

JOHN: But that's, that could never, they wouldn't let a—

MRS CLARK: What now?

(Beat)

JOHN: I had not considered.

MRS CLARK: I promise you, that if you—you—come ask her to vote, she will want you to give her someone to vote for. A person. Whom she knows. Who has eaten of the bread from her hands, yea, the bread that strengthenest men's hearts. That's from the Psalms, too. Let's take a break.

JOHN: The business about her education, what was that?

MRS CLARK: Everybody, what was that?

MAY: You made assumptions about who she was and what she'd done.

EMMA: If you're going to say your people are more successful than they look, you've got to believe it yourself.

JOHN: Come on, though, you had this country woman, studying in the Ivy League and getting a Master's degree. How likely is that?

MRS CLARK: Not very. Not very likely. Ooh, now I just want to go make me some biscuits! *(And she's gone, to check out the window.)*

(JOHN thinks for a moment.)

JOHN: She's done those things herself, hasn't she.

MR CARAWAN: Oh yeah.

MAY: You wanted to get taught. You got taught.

EMMA: It is a very nice suit, though.

NED: Okay. So. There is a problem with my organization.

(Beat)

(MRS CLARK crosses back and they reassemble.)

MRS CLARK: Go ahead.

NED: My problem is why people want to join my organization is because they're angry. It's not for what they want to do for themselves, it's for what they want to do to other people.

EMMA: What organization is this?

NED: Do I have to say? I didn't think we had to say.

MRS CLARK: It would help if we knew more specifics.

MAY: Is this the C I O?

NED: Sure. Yes. It doesn't matter what the group is. I know a lot of groups. People, they'll come to me and say, "We want to start something, you know how to start something, how do we start?" And I'll say, what's your problem, and they'll say, "It's those goddamn ..."

MRS CLARK: Those goddamn who?

JOHN: I think I know.

NED: It's different people. Over the years. It's all kinds of... Them. It's like there's always a new Them. But it's always the same talk.

MRS CLARK: Can we see that talk? Can you be that guy?

NED: I can be him. Who'll be me? Anybody?

MRS CLARK: Somebody will.

MR CARAWAN: I will.

NED: *(With an accent more country than his own)* It's like, *(Arms gesture: a big circle)* here's everything I would be. And here's *(Arms gesture: much smaller circle)* just who I actually get to be. And all the difference between is full of...

MR CARAWAN: Just say Those People. Just say Them. We'll know.

NED: Them. Standing in my place. Taking up my space. I see Them talking amongst themselves and laughing and I know they're laughing about me.

MR CARAWAN: So what is your real problem?

NED: It's Them.

MR CARAWAN: Is it though?

NED: Everybody else gets to point a finger, I can't point a finger?

MR CARAWAN: Do you want to solve the problem? Is pointing the finger enough?

NED: No.

MR CARAWAN: So what do you really want?

NED: I want Them to go away! I want them to go back down where they come from. I want them to go back to their place and out of mine.

MR CARAWAN: Whose place would be bigger, yours or theirs?

NED: Mine.

MR CARAWAN: Why?

NED: It's my place, my country, my ancestors, whoever had it before, wherever everybody was before, it belongs to my people now. Why are They here except to take what's ours?

MR CARAWAN: Why would They do that?

NED: Because that's what people do. They take. My people took from the red man when they had the chance and they made something better, the greatest country ever.

MR CARAWAN: Out of what they took.

NED: It's what everybody has always done but we just did it better.

MR CARAWAN: And what are you afraid of?

NED: That someone is doing the same thing to me.

MR CARAWAN: Is it possible to exert your rights without violating someone else's?

NED: I don't think anybody's done it yet.

MR CARAWAN: Is it possible for people to have equal rights?

NED: Not for long. That's how it always starts. That's never how it stays.

MR CARAWAN: But today, in all honesty, who has more power? You or Them?

NED: We have less than we did. There was a time when we had more than we do now, and everything was great.

MRS CLARK: And you say you've been having this talk since…

NED: As long as I can remember. Forever.

EMMA: And after this talk, what do you do?

NED: Somebody says, Let's go find one of Them and show 'em who's boss.

MRS CLARK: And who is boss?

NED: It's funny. At no other time are we boss. But we are boss, when we're showing Them.

MRS CLARK: And so your problem is?

NED: It doesn't fix anything. It never feels good for long. We don't know how to stop. And today it's us having this talk and doing these things. But someday it will be you. And I don't think you're going to do any better to solve it than us.

JOHN: That's about…Okay, step out. I'm going to be him.

MR CARAWAN: You want me to step out?

JOHN: No. (*To* NED) I'm going to be you.

NED: You're going to be me?

JOHN: Yeah yeah, We're here to share what we know. I know this man. I know you will correct me if I go wrong.

MRS CLARK: No mockery, please.

JOHN: An affectionate tribute to the other man's style. Like blackface. All in fun. We've endured a hundred years and more of blackface mockery. Indulge me for two minutes.

NED: Well all right. I yield the remainder of my time to the delegate from—where did you say you were from?

JOHN: This good ol' boy here is from Georgia. *(In NED's accent)* The Negro will vote when he is ready. When he has gained the sufficient sophistication and the intelligence through his continued education at the hands of the more developed races. *(Himself again)* All right, so now I'm stepping out. And who is steppin' in is this man from Baltimore... *(A white Maryland accent)* Our social welfare programs were designed with the common sense value that bearing children out of wedlock is a shame and a disgrace. As long as young Negro women see a baby as a meal ticket, I am not ready to spend my hard-earned tax dollars to subsidize a lifestyle of which I do not approve. I shouldn't have to do that. *(In his own voice)* And now stepping in is this man from Boston... *(South Boston accent)* I am not ready to have my children be the guinea pigs in a social experiment. To have to sit in a classroom with Negro children, having their progress slowed down by these Negro children, being exposed to the violence and sexuality of these Negro children. I am not ready for that. *(Himself once more)* Oh, and now stepping in is this man from Missouri... *(Missouri white voice)* There seems to be a fundamental criminality in the Negro character. I'm not saying all Negroes are criminals. The threat is always there. They do tend to take things that don't belong to them, or stand by while others do. Just look at the crime statistics. Why else would the arrests of Negroes be wildly out of proportion to their share of the population? What other possible reason could there be? *(Himself one last time)* And oh let's say...Florida. *(That voice)* He was coming toward me in an aggressive manner and I perceived a threat. He was obviously one of those thugs, one of those fatherless, drop-out, antisocial gangsters. So I stood my ground. I exercised my rights. I shot him. I'd do it again. *(Back to NED's Georgia drawl)* And my problem in my community is I keep having to buy more bullets. I keep not feeling safe. I keep feeling threatened. So I need to keep shooting and shooting and policing and jailing and failing and marginalizing and disenfranchising and ghettoizing and none of it is enough. I am so tired. My whipping arm is weary. What will it take for the Negro to understand how great I am? When oh when will the white man ever be free?

(Beat)

NED: What's your name again?

JOHN: I didn't say.

NED: Preacher's son, I think you said.

JOHN: My people don't know I'm here.

NED: Where'd you say you were from?

MRS CLARK: Hold on.

JOHN: I didn't say that either, Mr Ned Edwards.

MRS CLARK: Hold on.

JOHN: Of the Atlanta, Georgia C I O.

(NED lunges. JOHN is ready. The rest get between them.)

MRS CLARK: Damn it I said stop!

(Blackout)

END OF ACT ONE

ACT TWO

(The same moment. Everyone is still where they were.)

MRS CLARK: Damn it I said stop!

(Beat)

MR CARAWAN: *(To* JOHN*)* Is that what you really think of us? All of us?

JOHN: I am quoting y'all back to y'all, that's all. I know you're not all like that. But there does seem to be in the white man an inherent criminality. They do tend to take things that don't belong to them, or stand by while others do.

MR CARAWAN: Mrs Clark?

*(*MRS CLARK *turns to look out the window and down.)*

MR CARAWAN: Mrs Clark? May I bring you a glass of tea?

*(*MRS CLARK *shakes her head "no".)*

*(*NED *crosses away.)*

*(*MR CARAWAN *crosses to a phonograph.)*

*(*JOHN *approaches* MRS CLARK*.)*

JOHN: Showed them.

MRS CLARK: You sure did.

JOHN: I did.

MRS CLARK: Showed me, too. *(She crosses away.)*

JOHN: You wanted me to participate! This is me participating! *(He crosses away.)*

(MR CARAWAN fiddles with the phonograph.)

MAY: And after that we're just supposed to dance?

MR CARAWAN: After that we are just supposed to dance.

MAY: I may sit out the dancing.

EMMA: You could try.

MAY: I could fall on my face.

EMMA: And I don't know how, so we'll be even.

(Gradually, and gingerly, the others reassemble.)

(MRS CLARK, as always, goes to check the window.)

MAY: No, it's this leg, it's fine for walking, it just gives out now and then.

EMMA: What's the matter with your leg?

MAY: I got shot in it one time.

EMMA: Somebody shot you?

MAY: Just in the leg here. I can't be the only one—who else has got shot?

MR CARAWAN: Shot at.

NED: Shot at, sure.

MAY: So add that to my list of problems, I don't know how to get out of the way.

MR CARAWAN: Where did this happen?

MAY: I was walking a picket line, outside a knitting mill, here in Tennessee, and the owners had hired gun thugs, they were inside the mill, and they just started shooting. Five of us got shot.

MR CARAWAN: All in the legs?

MAY: I think.

MR CARAWAN: Shotgun or bullet?

MAY: Bullet.

MR CARAWAN: So what they were doing was they were shooting at the ground in front of you, so the bullets would ricochet off and hit you all low. They wanted to scare you off.

MAY: Then they made a mistake. But you know who they did scare off? They carried me home, with this leg, and I wanted to see my kids. Where are my kids? And my husband stands at the foot of the bed and says, "Darlin', you have got to stop doing things like this." And I'm all, "They shot me, you get that *they* shot *me*?" And he says, "The doctor says he believes that you are not well adjusted to life."

NED: Company doctor?

MAY: Company doctor says I am clearly a very troubled person. I said, "Where are my kids?" His mom took the two oldest, one girl's with his sister, my sister's got the baby, and that is how they are going to be. From now on. I was fighting for them. But it seems like being the kind of person who can put up a fight means I can't...

(Beat)

EMMA: Where's your husband now?

MAY: I cannot say for sure, but I truly do hope that he is in Hell. They are all scattered to the wind. Well, that's my tale of woe, I bet everybody's got one, nothing special about mine. Who's next?

MRS CLARK: And hold on. You all see what she did? You can use your story to make yourself special or you can use it to make a connection. You're blacklisted in Kentucky.

MAY: That's right. *(To* EMMA*)* And you got kicked out of Texas.

EMMA: That's right.

MRS CLARK: And I am no longer welcome in South Carolina. Which means really? We never were. You can be born and raised in a place and never welcome in it.

MAY: If you are not well adjusted to life.

MRS CLARK: Sometimes you have to hear someone else's story to understand your own.

EMMA: I do miss it, though.

MAY: Sure.

MRS CLARK: What do you miss? What do your people love? Everybody. We talk a lot about what we fight against. What will your people fight for?

EMMA: I miss my home that's gone.

NED: These woods remind me of our woods.

JOHN: Your woods?

NED: The woods my family had always hunted in. We'd grow vegetables in the kitchen garden, keep chickens and a hog, but those woods give us greens, mushrooms

MR CARAWAN: Squirrel coon rabbit

MAY: Deer, one'll last you the winter for meat

EMMA: There were streams ran through ours

NED: That'll give you fish we called them croppies where I'm from

MRS CLARK: Crawdads

JOHN: Frogs

NED: You ever been gigging frogs

JOHN: We kids'd spear them with sticks

MAY: Bring 'em home to give your mama

MRS CLARK: Catfish, my mama's

JOHN: No my mama's catfish

EMMA: One time my brother and me caught a fish it took two of us to carry home

MR CARAWAN: My mama filleted them

EMMA: Flat of her hand on the fish on the table

MAY: Mine would like she was shaking hands

EMMA: And that sharp sharp knife

NED: Oh my mama's boning knife

JOHN: I was scared of that knife

NED: I'm still scared of my mama's boning knife

MR CARAWAN: My daddy was scared of that knife

MRS CLARK: Two white men came by one time, they'd caught a glimpse of my sister, my mama snatched up that knife and those white men were laughing like the whole thing was a joke but they backed away.

MAY: Lord have mercy.

MRS CLARK: Not here to complain, here to work. How's your mama do her catfish?

JOHN: Mine dips them in buttermilk rolls them in corn meal

EMMA: Fry them in the iron skillet

NED: When your family sits down to a meal that you caught

MAY: My grandma showed me where the tenderest greens

NED: You're a young man that day

MR CARAWAN: Those woods provided

MAY: Who you were going to be

JOHN: Why would you want to be anyone else than who you were in those woods and at that table?

EMMA: All of that provided by land that

MR CARAWAN: We have always worked that land

NED: As far back as anyone can remember

MRS CLARK: Land that as it turns out

EMMA: We did not own.

NED: Strangers bought our land and we never saw any money

JOHN: We had no say and if you spoke up you'd be killed

MAY: Men with weapons came and pushed us out

MR CARAWAN: They said can you prove this land belongs to you?

EMMA: What are you doing here?

NED: We have a deed.

EMMA: A treaty.

MAY: A contract.

JOHN: A law.

MR CARAWAN: We have title. Do you have title?

NED: We have big plans for all this here.

MRS CLARK: There is a war. You are prisoners. You belong to us now.

EMMA: You have to go.

JOHN: You have to come with us.

MAY: And it turns out our woods was owned by

NED: The American Coal Company, based in London, England

MR CARAWAN: The United Fruit Company, based in New York City

JOHN: And we all had to go

NED: So you go where the work is.

MAY: Now you work for wages.

EMMA: And whose money is it? Who makes it? The same people who took your place. Who else has money and work they want done?

JOHN: They take you where the work is.

EMMA: Now you work for them.

MRS CLARK: But you tell your children, once we had a place of our own.

(Beat)

NED: There are times I just— *(Fist into hand)* Don't you ever want to—

MR CARAWAN: I've been hit.

NED: Me too. How I was raised? I needed to be hit.

MR CARAWAN: I don't think anybody needs to be hit.

NED: You didn't know me. I'm not going to stand here and say they didn't raise me right.

MR CARAWAN: I don't think I'm perfect. But I don't want to be that kind of man, that hitting man. When he's hitting, look at his face. I'd rather be me than be that.

MAY: Sometimes you have to.

MR CARAWAN: Maybe somebody does. Some people are good at that kind of thing. Just not me.

JOHN: Sometimes scaring people is a way to do them a favor. All of us know people on our own side who would be fine just killing people outright. Like cleansing a stain. They don't see people who are different from them as human beings at all.

MRS CLARK: Just devils. Mm hm.

EMMA: That's right. Animals.

JOHN: So if somebody does something that just…warns people. That what they are doing or saying is putting them in danger of some sort of righteous retribution.

NED: That somebody is actually being a friend.

JOHN: Real helpful like.

NED: Yeah. I think we understand each other.

JOHN: I think we do.

NED: Has anybody told you anything about me?

JOHN: Nobody has to tell me anything about you.

MRS CLARK: What are you two doing?

NED: We are agreeing that all this pacifism that Mr Carawan is talking about only works if there is the threat of violence behind it.

MAY: I'm armed right now. Aren't you?

MRS CLARK: Hold on. All this needed to be said. This is what I hear: every one of our communities has a story and a grudge about every other one. Your people were scabs against your people and your people hunted your people and the men did this to the women and the women, well, we must have done something.

EMMA: We're crazy.

MAY: And badly adjusted to life.

MRS CLARK: So if we are all so at odds—did you hear each other? —Why were you able to finish each other's sentences? How could you read each other's thoughts?

(Beat)

EMMA: We were telling the same story.

MRS CLARK: To a very large degree.

JOHN: I cannot agree completely.

MRS CLARK: No. We cannot. But.

JOHN: *(With difficulty)* But I do see that the experience of colonization is one that, in some way, all our communities...share.

MRS CLARK: I see you, holding me up. I thank you. Everybody's got their particular tale. But what you were saying. Are you the reason for each other's troubles? Your people, your people?

JOHN: The problem is— *(To* MAY*)* Like you said before—you never get to fight the men who give the orders. They send drunks and convicts and guys who think a uniform will make them men. They give them money and buy them drinks and hand them weapons. They say you have the legal right and if you want it the moral obligation to beat the crap out of people like you and me.

MR CARAWAN: I just...I want to say something about my problem. We're talking a lot about the danger of being hurt by violence. Has anybody here had to kill anyone?

NED: Hunting.

MAY: Deer, sure.

NED: Going up into the woods with my dad.

MR CARAWAN: That's not what I'm talking about. Who's been in the military?

(All the men raise their hands.)

NED: Drafted, sure.

MR CARAWAN: Where were you stationed?

JOHN: Japan.

NED: West Berlin.

MR CARAWAN: Panama. So nobody was in Korea, nobody saw combat. Were you okay carrying a gun?

NED: I was used to it, hunting.

MR CARAWAN: I found I hated carrying a gun. When you have a gun, you cannot believe anything anyone tells you. They will say whatever they need to so that you will not hurt them.

JOHN: They were glad we were there. They told us so. How grateful they were.

MR CARAWAN: Did you have guns?

JOHN: We were soldiers.

MR CARAWAN: They told you what they thought you wanted to hear.

JOHN: Oh. Like growing up in the South. You're taught, whatever you do, don't talk back.

NED: Now...

(Beat)

MRS CLARK: Go ahead. This conversation had to happen.

NED: My grandfather says he grew up side by side with Negro children. They all got along, they understood each other, they loved each other.

JOHN: Did your grandfather's family have guns?

NED: Everybody did, it was the country.

JOHN: The sheriffs, the police—were they white or Black?

NED: They were white.

JOHN: Was there Ku Klux Klan in the area? White Citizens Council? Had there been any lynchings in your county?

NED: Sure.

JOHN: Those happy Negroes were performing at gunpoint. And a statue, by the way, the statues they have been putting up lately all over the South, with a gun or a sword, those are a kind of scarecrow. They're a warning. "We've done it before, we're proud we did. We can do it again. Now, do you love us?" Why, yes, yes, Bossman, of course we do.

MR CARAWAN: If you have to come armed to a conversation, you're saying you don't trust the people you're with.

MAY: I'm just protecting myself.

MR CARAWAN: Sure. But you will never know the truth.

MAY: I can live with that.

NED: The soldiers in my family are the most honorable people I know.

EMMA: Ask the women how honorable they are. Ask the women of the countries they've occupied.

NED: We treat them better than their own men.

EMMA: How do you know that?

NED: They told us again and again.

EMMA: Were you armed at the time? *(Beat)* "I am so grateful you're here, with your gun. You are so much better than those other men with guns, the men of my own people." People will say what they need to. If they are sensible.

NED: So why are you telling me this?

EMMA: I am not a sensible person.

MR CARAWAN: Maybe it's true, maybe it's not. The point is, you will never know. This is hard for me to say. I was proud to join up. The men who fought the fascists, I had so much admiration. But when I was stationed in Central America, the places where villages had been, there were factory farms. They weren't owned by the people of those countries. They were just like the…

EMMA: Oil fields.

NED: Mining operations.

MAY: They cleared every field and tree.

MR CARAWAN: The men who own the United Fruit Company, who own the land where I was stationed, are the same men who sit on the board of the American Coal Company. Literally the same men, the same handful of families. And I was there to do the exact same thing that had been done to my family, for the exact same people. I was a gun thug.

MRS CLARK: Hold on. You did the first thing we can do. You learned something. All of you, your people can do research, they can look things up, they can learn the names of who they're fighting. It is not faceless forces, or an Invisible Hand, or the will of the Almighty. It is just some people.

MAY: But you can never get to them. You can never…

MRS CLARK: You can never shoot them back. So there must be another way. But the thing—do you hear what she did again? You are something. She knows—you know—the man who shot you isn't who shot you. The man who shot you is the man who bought the gun.

(Beat)

NED: So when people say you're a Communist training school…

MRS CLARK: Anybody who wants to change things gets called a Communist. Mr Horton likes to say we don't want Communism, we want something way more radical than that. We want a democracy. Now, I keep

hearing there's going to be dancing. I'm washing up
and then I expect to be dancing.

(They head off in various directions.)

(Except for MAY *and* EMMA, *who start clearing away the
chairs.)*

EMMA: Ask you a question?

MAY: Sure.

EMMA: Are we pretending nothing happened?

MAY: Why would we want to do that?

EMMA: Okay. Good. What?

MAY: I've never known anybody like you.

EMMA: Crap.

MAY: What?

EMMA: Like me how?

MAY: Who's from wherever you're from.

EMMA: Oh. *Tejas.*

MAY: But before that.

EMMA: *Tejas.*

MAY: But before that.

EMMA: I keep saying, my people were in *Tejas* before it
was Texas.

MAY: But you have an accent.

EMMA: You have an accent.

MAY: Well, hell, that's true. Did I piss you off?

EMMA: Look. I've met lots of people like you. I don't
want to get to know somebody like you. I want to
know you. Maybe. If you would stop pissing me off.

MAY: I piss plenty of people off. That doesn't make you
special.

EMMA: Why?

MAY: Why do I piss people off? I don't know. Just being me. How did I piss you off?

EMMA: Don't ask me about the kind of person I am. Ask about me.

MAY: I know I'm ignorant. I don't even know…is there some story about the kind of person you are? Some way you're all—whichever all you are—is supposed to be?

EMMA: What do you mean?

MAY: I mean everybody knows what they're supposed to think about somebody like me. I'm a redneck hillbilly mountain girl from up the holler, inbred, rickety, dumb as dirt.

EMMA: But you're not like that.

MAY: None of us is like that! Nobody I know is like what everybody says! Okay, I've got a couple of cousins. But I'm saying, whatever everybody thinks about you, that you know isn't true? I'm so ignorant of you that I don't even know what those things are.

EMMA: What are you trying to ask me?

MAY: I'm asking you, don't give up on me! Please! If I could just know you, before I knew about you, before I learn what everybody thinks.

EMMA: What would you do? What would you want to do?

MAY: I would want to just know each other.

EMMA: Maybe we could do that.

MAY: And wasn't there going to be dancing? Maybe I might try dancing.

THE SQUARE DANCE

(They dance. MR CARAWAN *starts the phonograph, then joins, calling helpful instructive calls for the benefit of those who haven't done this before.)*

(They dance. MRS CLARK, *and* NED *know how. The others have to pick it up, and, with help, they do.)*

(Everyone is aware, as they switch partners and link arms, that they are doing something unprecedented and illegal: dancing with people of races other than their own.)

(They start slowly, tentatively, with a kind of exaggerated courtliness.)

(But very soon they are doing the things people do when they are caught up in a dance: moving with pleasure, making eye contact, trying moves, cheering the moves each other try.)

(In all the excitement, no one is looking out the window or listening for sounds outside.)

(We hear car engines. We see the beams of headlights, first one set, then two. A horn sounds.)

(Then the dancers know something is wrong. They break from each other and glance around for the source of the threat.)

(More sets of headlights shine up at them. Headlights appear, disappear, more from different directions.)

(There is a shot. Laughter. Shouting)

(The dancers look around and move to escape.)

VOICE: Stop! Do not move! Hands in the air!

MRS CLARK: Who are you? Are you the police?

VOICE: Who's in charge?

MRS CLARK: What do you want?

VOICE: We hear there's drinking and dancing going on up here.

MRS CLARK: I don't drink. If you were looking for a drinking party, you've come to the wrong place.

VOICE: Are you aware that this is a dry county?

NED: We know!!!

MRS CLARK: We are not drinking.

VOICE: Seems like you're running a dance hall up here.

MRS CLARK: This is a school.

VOICE: Where's your desks? Where's your children?

MRS CLARK: It's a school for adults.

VOICE: No, you've got a dance hall up here where white men can drink and dance with colored girls.

MRS CLARK: You lie!

MR CARAWAN: Mrs Clark, don't get shot.

MRS CLARK: I am not a drinking woman! I am not some bad woman running dances for white men!

MR CARAWAN: Mrs Clark! Please don't get shot!

MRS CLARK: These men are going to shoot me or not but they are not going to throw dirt on my good name! You hear me? I will not have that from you!

NED: You're going to get us killed.

MAY: They can't kill all of us all the time.

VOICE: Sit your ass back down!

MRS CLARK: This is a school! I'm a school teacher. What are you?

VOICE: What are you teaching up here then? Huh? What are you teaching?

MR CARAWAN: Singing!

VOICE: Singing?

MR CARAWAN: It's a singing school.

(MR CARAWAN *sings.* MRS CLARK *joins. They all sing,
shakily but loudly.*)

ALL:
We shall not, we shall not be moved
We shall not, we shall not be moved
Just like a tree, planted by the water
We shall not be moved

MR CARAWAN: *(Speaking)* We are not afraid.

ALL:
We are not, we are not afraid
We are not, we are not afraid
Just like a tree, planted by the water
We are not afraid.

(A gunshot. Lights out.)

*(It is mostly dark and it is not clear where they are, but they
are in two clumps, the men in one place and the women,
separately lit, in another. At this point we only see the men.)*

NED: *(Gleeful)* Well. Well well well well. The cavalry is
here.

MR CARAWAN: We've got no time.

NED: You boys are going to get educated now, I bet.

MR CARAWAN: Seriously, shut up. *(To* JOHN*)* We've got
to make sure you get through this.

JOHN: I'll do this on my own, thanks.

MR CARAWAN: Nobody gets through a thing like this
on his own. Whether they came in costume or not,
those men are Klan. Listen to me or don't, but here's
what I know. Don't surprise them. Give them a way
out. They'll be looking at each other. It's a test. How
they treat you is their loyalty oath. Get one of them to
laugh. One of them has to decide to treat the whole
thing and you as a joke.

JOHN: I will not clown.

NED: You've been clowning since you got here.

MR CARAWAN: It will not be you doing it. Whatever
show you need to put on, the real you will be back
here, right here. Your only job is to get out of this
alive. You have no moral obligation to tell the truth to
someone holding you at gunpoint. These men do not
care about the truth. They are self-pitying drunks with
guns. That's all. Now, have you had to take a beating
before? A whupping from your daddy doesn't count.

JOHN: In the service I did some brawling.

MR CARAWAN: You'll be outnumbered, but you can
take a beating and survive. Turtle down. Protect your
body. Curl up, so your internal organs don't take the
blows. Try to maintain eye contact.

JOHN: What's that for?

MR CARAWAN: Reminds them you're a fellow human
being. They probably won't hit your head or chest—
that can kill you and they mostly don't need to kill us.
They want us to come away so we're crippled but we
don't die.

NED: But sometimes a man gets carried away.

MR CARAWAN: Help them not to get carried away.
What else? Along with being Klan, they may also be
cops. If you even raise your hand to defend yourself,
it's assaulting an officer. And the big point—we don't
have time! But—look, it's not enough not to hit back.
You can't *want* to hit back. You have to want *not* to hit
back. You have to love that person who's hitting you.

JOHN: Oh for fuck's sake.

NED: You are shitting me.

MR CARAWAN: I know, it's nuts, I can't do it yet. But
when he's cursing at you, spitting on you, pushing
lit cigarettes into your neck—if you can find a way to

feel that he's a victim too, that the same forces you're fighting have made him this angry, this scared of what will happen to him if we win. Then you will win. You will be nonviolent.

JOHN: You would have to be Jesus Christ.

NED: And look what they did to him.

MR CARAWAN: When I said you can take a beating and survive, that is what I mean. If we get out of this, I've got to remember to tell Mrs Clark we need to cover this on day one.

NED: I guess I still don't understand what you said about the Klan.

MR CARAWAN: I told you at the start, this is a sundown county. Any Negro who has tried to live in this county has been driven out or killed.

NED: Mrs Clark lives here.

MR CARAWAN: Yes she does. I don't pray very much anymore. Not like I should. But what I do is, every day that I can, I bring a glass of tea to Mrs Clark.

(A sudden brighter light on the men, which fades as lights come up on the women.)

EMMA: You'll be okay. You'll be okay.

MAY: Why would you think I'll be okay?

EMMA: *(To MRS CLARK)* It's you I'm worried about.

MRS CLARK: Don't worry about me.

MAY: Here. *(She holds out a clasp knife.)*

MRS CLARK: What good do you think that will do?

MAY: You told that story, your mother and her knife and those men.

MRS CLARK: Different situation.

MAY: What do you think they want?

EMMA: They're a pack of drunk men.

MRS CLARK: They're out for revenge.

EMMA: They're looking for whores.

MRS CLARK: Like I said.

MAY: Do you want the knife?

EMMA: No. If they think we are whores they will rape us and leave a couple of dollars and claim it was business. Haven't you ever even heard stories like that?

MAY: I have, I guess, I just…

EMMA: You thought the men were telling the truth. Didn't you.

MAY: I have to live with men like this.

MRS CLARK: They will ask you if John has said or done anything to you. You must be absolutely careful and consistent with your answer. No matter what they call you.

MAY: Why?

EMMA: You cannot be this ignorant!

MAY: Please!

MRS CLARK: Because if you even suggest that you two have had anything—anything! —to do with each other, they will lynch him.

MAY: But I haven't. I wouldn't.

MRS CLARK: Are you sure?

MAY: No. Yes. No, I mean, yes I'm sure, no I wouldn't.

EMMA: No?

MAY: God no.

MRS CLARK: Why not?

MAY: (To EMMA) You know why not.

MRS CLARK: Is it because he's Black?

(Beat)

EMMA: It's because he's a man.

MAY: No. What? I've been married.

MRS CLARK: Well?

MAY: *(To* EMMA*)* It's because he's not you!

MRS CLARK: Say it's because he's Black. Say you scarcely noticed he was here.

MAY: What will he say?

MRS CLARK: He will say the same.

MAY: Are you sure?

MRS CLARK: He has been trained to give that answer since he was a child.

MAY: *(Holding out the knife to* EMMA*)* Do you want this?

EMMA: They already think I'm a whore. They'll expect me to have a knife.

MAY: Why?

EMMA: Because I'm *Mexicana.* You ignorant hick.

MAY: I thought you were American.

EMMA: I am American! I am Mexican American! But that is a distinction you people are too damn stupid to make! So keep your knife, and try not to say something stupid that will get people killed.

MAY: I wouldn't do that.

EMMA: That is what always happens. Some white girl starts crying, saying "I didn't do anything. It wasn't me. None of this is my fault."

MRS CLARK: Hold on.

EMMA: And your men say, "Whose fault was it then?" And somebody dies. And it's never you.

MRS CLARK: Hold on.

EMMA: Now stop your damn tears. They are lethal.

MRS CLARK: Hold ON.

EMMA: Am I wrong?

MRS CLARK: You're not wrong. You're not helping. Keep it simple. *(To* MAY*)* What are you going to say?

MAY: I'm going to say I never really got to know anybody up here. I never said anything much to anybody and nobody said much to me.

EMMA: That's right.

MRS CLARK: Will they believe you?

MAY: Sure they will. That's all they expect of me. So you don't want this?

EMMA: Why don't you want it yourself? Why do you keep wanting to give it to me?

MAY: You think I only carry one weapon? *(She turns away.)*

*(*MRS CLARK *looks at* EMMA, *long.)*

MRS CLARK: You treat all your women like that? Or just the white ones?

EMMA: Not your business, Mrs Clark.

MRS CLARK: You are in my schoolroom. You are my business.

EMMA: I'm not wrong.

MRS CLARK: But you did wrong. That woman deserves nothing but kindness and respect. Especially from you.

EMMA: We—

MRS CLARK: This is outside my experience and not a subject I care to discuss. But please. A child could tell what you are to each other.

(Beat)

EMMA: When I was in jail in San Antonio, it felt so long,
I got so sad, but I wasn't afraid. I just thought about
justice. That's what I told people. But it was cold at
night. I was thinking about those men who sang to us.
It helped. *(Singing quietly)*
De colores, de colores
Se visten los campos en la primavera.
De colores, de colores
Son los pajaritos que vienen de afuera.

*(*EMMA, *joined by* MRS CLARK, *then* MAY*)*

EMMA, MRS CLARK, MAY:
De colores, de colores

EMMA:
Es el arco iris que vemos lucir.
Y por eso los grandes amores
De muchos colores me gustan a mí.
Y por eso los grandes amores
De muchos colores me gustan a mí.

MRS CLARK: Are y'all okay?

MAY: I'll be okay.

MRS CLARK: You're crying again.

MAY: Well, you're crying, too.

MRS CLARK: *(To* EMMA*)* What does that mean?

EMMA: It's about the colors. Loving all the colors.

MAY: You think okay, I'm just sad, I'll just always be
sad. And then something happens, and you're happy
for a moment and it hurts.

MRS CLARK: This is why at Highlander we make
everybody sing a lot of songs. You must not tell this to
a living soul, especially not to Mr Clark, And especially
not to Mr Carawan. But I am very fond of Mr Carawan,
when he sings.

EMMA: We're going to get out of this.

MAY: Fight another day.

(A brighter light on the women, which then goes out.)

(Then, one by one, they are each standing or sitting or kneeling in isolation. They are being questioned. We do not hear the questions, only their responses.)

(MR CARAWAN stands at attention and recites, loudly.)

MR CARAWAN: Article 1: I am an American, fighting in the forces which guard my country and our way of life. I am prepared to give my life in their defense.
Article 2: I will never surrender of my own free will. If in command I will never surrender the members of my command while they still have the means to resist.

EMMA: No, it is not a Communist school. No, they are not affiliated with the Communist Party. You want to know how I know, I will tell you how I know, because I was a Communist. For a couple of months. We were never going to work out. But the Communists fed my people when they were starving in this country, I am not going to renounce them now. But the Communist Party demands total obedience. These guys are all over the place. They would be the worst Communists ever.

MR CARAWAN: Article 3: If I am captured I will continue to resist by all means available. I will make every effort to escape and aid others to escape. I will accept neither parole nor special favors from the enemy.

(MAY crouches in a defensive posture.)

MAY: I will kill the first one who touches me. I am armed. You can shoot me from over there, but the first one who comes close, I will take with me. So there are four of you and you need to figure out which one dies first. You'll need to organize yourselves. You want to try one at a time, or a pair of you? Talk it over. I have children by the way, I'm just saying I'm used to being

ACT TWO 75

outnumbered. You got kids? Yeah, we've got kids.
What's it going to take for us all to get home to our
kids, and look 'em in the eye? Huh? Well?

MR CARAWAN: Article 4: If I become a prisoner of war,
I will keep faith with my fellow prisoners. I will give
no information or take part in any action which might
be harmful to my comrades. If I am senior, I will take
command. If not, I will obey the lawful orders of those
appointed over me and will back them up in every
way.

NED: Well, hey, hey, howdy, fellas, am I glad to see
you. I am up here from the flatlands and I hear tell
there is nothing finer than that Tennessee sipping
whiskey. And I do believe you have plenty with you
tonight. Tell me you haven't drunk it all? Because I am
parched. I've been dreaming about that moonshine. I
know every one of y'all's got a still hidden away up the
holler. What do you say this Georgia cracker and you
hillbillies have us a party! *(Beat)* Crap.

MR CARAWAN: Article 5: When questioned, should
I become a prisoner of war, I am required to give
name, rank, service number, and date of birth. I will
evade answering further questions to the utmost of
my ability. I will make no oral or written statements
disloyal to my country and its allies or harmful to their
cause.

JOHN: Yes, sir. Yes, sir. Oh, I'm just here—yes, that's
my car, I did drive here in that car. The suit? See, I can
explain all that, I am here simply…I'se just here. To be
driving Mister Edwards. That's right, sir. I don't really
know what all they're talking about, that's not my
business. I think it's a kind of Bible school. They sing a
lot of hymns, and they talk about people not fighting
with each other, and giving to the poor. Welcoming
the stranger. Comforting those imprisoned. Giving up

your riches to save your soul, and not judging who's a sinner and who's not, you know, all the things that Christians believe and do.

MR CARAWAN: Article 6: I will never forget that I am an American, fighting for freedom, responsible for my actions, and dedicated to the principles which made my country free. I will trust in my God and in the United States of America.

DAY THREE

(The center of the stage is empty. The chairs, which had been pushed aside for dancing, are tossed aside still.)

(MAY enters, with a suitcase, and studies the room. She crosses to a chair, picks it up and carries it to its place. She stands by it for a moment. Then she goes to get another chair and does it again.)

(EMMA comes in, with a suitcase, and sees. She picks up a chair and sets it. They keep setting the chairs in what becomes a circle.)

EMMA: I did wrong. I was scared and I did wrong.

MAY: I was scared too. I don't know why you got scared at me.

EMMA: I wasn't just scared of the men. You don't know what it's like.

MAY: What?

EMMA: To live this life.

MAY: I know I don't know. But this is a school.

EMMA: It's a school where people do a lot of pretending.

MAY: I'm not pretending anything. You're the one who doesn't understand. You've done things all over, known all kinds of people, but...

EMMA: What?

MAY: I didn't know there was anyone else that felt like me. I thought I was the only one.

(Beat)

EMMA: There are plenty of us. Now that you know, you'll see us everywhere.

MAY: This is the craziest school, I feel like I know less than when I got here.

EMMA: Remember I told you I dreamed about you.

MAY: I wouldn't forget a thing like that.

EMMA: I feel like...I want to run into a burning building with you, and save somebody. I dreamed that. And then we came out of the fire all covered in soot, carrying sooty children. And the children squirmed out of our arms and ran to their families and everyone was cheering for us and then we were kissing. We were kissing and people started cheering even louder, which makes no sense in all the world, and then we were old, and I was yours, and you were mine. And every time I look at you...

MAY: It sounds like a good dream. To me.

EMMA: But then I woke up, and thought of everything that would keep it from happening and that scared me so much it was just easier to keep it from happening by getting mad at you.

(MRS CLARK enters.)

MRS CLARK: You two—

EMMA: Mrs Clark.

MAY: Good morning.

MRS CLARK: Good morning. You might want to keep all this to yourselves.

EMMA: I'm sorry, we're—

MRS CLARK: You're trying to figure some things out. While you do, please remember where you are.

EMMA: We will.

MAY: Mrs Clark. I thought we're in a place where people learn who their people are, and what they want.

(MR CARAWAN *enters, with the tea tray, and crosses to* MRS CLARK.)

MR CARAWAN: Good morning, Mrs Clark.

MRS CLARK: Good morning, Mr Carawan.

MR CARAWAN: Glass of tea?

MRS CLARK: You are kindness itself.

(JOHN *enters, carrying a suitcase, and sits.*)

(*They sit together in silence for a moment.*)

JOHN: Did you ever find out who they were?

MRS CLARK: Who they always are. Sometimes they come with badges, sometimes they come with hoods. Sometimes they come with gasoline and torches.

EMMA: I was afraid they were going to lynch somebody.

MRS CLARK: They didn't lynch anybody because they didn't think they needed to.

EMMA: Or burn the place down.

MRS CLARK: They could have. They still might. They could burn the buildings. But they can't burn Highlander. Highlander's in idea. You can't burn down an idea.

(NED *enters, carrying a suitcase, visibly bruised.*)

NED: Man, those mountain boys hit hard. Turns out "hillbilly" is not a word they like to hear. Somebody could have told me that. I've heard you use it.

MAY: We get to use it. Not you.

NED: So I did learn something up here.

MRS CLARK: It seems you did. When those men were questioning me, they said someone here had told them he was a spy, a very important spy, spying on communist activity, and they had better let him go because he had to make his report.

(Beat)

JOHN: Report to whom?

MRS CLARK: The C I O? F B I? K K K? Who do you report to, Ned?

NED: I report to the C I O.

MRS CLARK: And?

NED: And where the report goes from there is not for me to know. But the C I O is going to cut you off. This whole place is a bad idea. You have never made anything happen, any of you, and you never will. The Klan, at least, accomplishes what it sets out to do. Lord, my head hurts.

MRS CLARK: I'm disappointed. I was hoping you might become one of our successes.

NED: I don't want to be your success. Do you think this is an idea anybody wants? That this is what the future ought to be? Compelled into close quarters with all kinds of people I don't know. Can't say anything, can't do anything. My freedom will be gone.

JOHN: Yes, that would be terrible.

NED: I know, I know, you think that's how you live now. Well then, that's what you deserve. I am freer than you and I aim to keep it that way. Look, I know you're not the goddamn card-carrying Red Russian army. You don't need to be. They work for you. But you all don't know, can't even tell, that I am not—a man like me—is not, am not, nor have I ever been, a member of the Ku Klux Klan!

JOHN: You don't need to be. They work for you.

(NED *heads out, but turns back.*)

NED: If you wanted to know if a group of people like this can work together, the answer is no! (*He exits.*)

MR CARAWAN: Mrs Clark? How are you?

MRS CLARK: Last night I was afraid. I don't mind confessing. Then I realized those men figured that all I was, all I could possibly be, was up here to cook and clean and be caretaking for you all. Which I want to believe I am. Caretaking. But that I could be responsible for all this was so far outside those men's conception that it never entered their pointy little minds.

MAY: Thank God.

MRS CLARK: I let them keep thinking that. I could have educated them, and I did not. So that's on me.

MR CARAWAN: Better another time.

MRS CLARK: Better another time.

JOHN: What happens now?

MRS CLARK: On the final day of a workshop, we do something called "Finding Your Way Back Home." We ask everyone to say how they're going to use what they learned back in their home community.

MAY: Well. I just figured something out.

MRS CLARK: What's that?

MAY: *(To* EMMA*)* So there are people? All over? Who have to pretend they don't even exist? And you, too?

EMMA: Yes.

MAY: Well, that's not fair. That's not fair at all.

EMMA: No.

MAY: Somebody ought to do something.

EMMA: Like what?

MAY: I don't...but...this is a problem. If nobody even knows...They should know.

EMMA: Know what?

MAY: That we're here.

JOHN: Excuse me, but what are you—

MRS CLARK: Hold on. *(To* EMMA *and* MAY*)* Go ahead.

MAY: What did you say, the other day, about a demonstration?

EMMA: That's politics, we're not talking about politics.

MAY: Honey. We sure as hell are. Aren't we?

EMMA: A demonstration...I don't remember what I said.

MAY: A demonstration is teaching someone something by showing them how it works. And to do that...what did you say?

EMMA: Sometimes you have to make a spectacle of yourself. *Ay, mierda.*

*(*EMMA *and* MAY *show that if they are at the beginning of six decades of political work, it will be, as* MAY *said two long days ago, an act of love. They pick up their suitcases, take hands, and head for the door.)*

MRS CLARK: Well then. Let us know how Highlander can help.

(EMMA *and* MAY *depart together. Beat)*

JOHN: What just happened?

MRS CLARK: I think I just got taught something. Everybody's right, this is the craziest kind of school.

JOHN: If Highlander remains open, do you plan to continue as Education Director?

MRS CLARK: I do not know that I am up to this work.

JOHN: Really? On the contrary, I believe you to be… *(To* MR CARAWAN*)* You were in the service. You know the expression, the H M F I C?

MR CARAWAN: I do know the expression. H M F I C. That is just the right job title.

MRS CLARK: Well, I wasn't in the service and I don't know what you all are talking about. What is the H M F I C?

(Beat)

JOHN: Head MuthaFucka In Charge.

*(*MR CARAWAN *tiptoes out.)*

MRS CLARK: That is a deeply inappropriate use of language! Will you ever stop embarrassing me? *(She cannot keep a straight face any longer.)* H M F I C…

*(*JOHN *laughs.* MRS CLARK *glares. He stops.)*

JOHN: It seems you will have some spaces available in your upcoming workshops.

MRS CLARK: There may not be any more workshops. That was almost all our money walking out the door. How am I going to tell Mr Horton what I did to his school? I was going to say I don't know how we'll keep the doors open, but they busted down the doors last night.

JOHN: I hope there will be a next workshop. We will be
more than happy to foot the bill. And buy you some
new doors.

MRS CLARK: We?

JOHN: The N A A C P. I am an elected officer of the N
A A C P, in Alabama. I had heard about this place, but
I wanted to see for myself how it works. It works very
well.

MRS CLARK: What works?

JOHN: Your school. Your whole approach. And you,
Mrs Clark. You've got to know...I have never met a
better teacher. Now. I'm going to put some people in
touch, to make arrangements for them to come here
and learn from you. Let's start with our Montgomery
chapter, I think, they have worked for years to fight
Jim Crow, with no success. They are understandably
discouraged. But you, Mrs Clark, and this place, have
a way of lighting a fire under people. What you are
making here is like no place else in all the South. You'll
be hearing from the Secretary of our Montgomery
chapter.

MRS CLARK: I will look for his letter. What is his name?

JOHN: Her name is Mrs Parks, Mrs Rosa Parks. I believe
she could learn a lot from you. I know I have.(*He exits.*)

MRS CLARK: Well now. Well now. Oh my goodness,
and we didn't even sing. At the Highlander Folk
School, we start the day singing. (*Singing*)
Paul and Silas bound in jail
Got no money for to go their bail
Keep your hand on the plow, go on

Paul and Silas started to shout
Walls bust open and they all walked out
Keep your hand on the plow, hold on

(MR CARAWAN *enters.*)

MRS CLARK & MR CARAWAN:
Hold on, hold on
Keep your hand on that plow, go on

(EMMA *and* MAY *enter.*)

MAY: In Kentucky it goes like this. *(Singing)*
Got my hands on the gospel plow
Wouldn't take nothin' for my journey now
Keep your hands on the plow of God

EMMA, MAY, MRS CLARK & MR CARAWAN:
Hold on, hold on
Keep your hands on that plow, hold on

(JOHN *enters.*)

MR CARAWAN: Mrs Alice Wines sings it like this.
(Singing)
I never been to heaven but I've been told

MR CARAWAN & JOHN
It's a first-class city and it's paved with gold.
Keep your eyes on the prize, go on

ALL:
Go on, go on
Keep your eyes on the prize, go on

The only thing that we did wrong
Was stay in the wilderness too long
Keep your eyes on the prize, go on

The only day that we did right
Was the day we started to fight
Keep your eyes on the prize, go on

Go on, go on
Keep your eyes on the prize, go on

MRS CLARK: *(To the audience)* You all know it by now.
Join in!

(*Even* NED *enters, freed from his character.*)

ALL:
Go on, go on
Keep your eyes on the prize, go on

Go on, go on
Keep your eyes on the prize,
Go on.

END OF PLAY